2

Covenant Power Today:
The Divine Connection

NICHOLAS KISAKYE, PETER ASIIMWE

KHAMEL
PUBLISHING

ISBN: 978-9970-9453-6-8
© 2016 Nicholas Kisakye / Peter Ruhukya Asiimwe
Second edition.
First published in 2011.

Author Contact:
Return to Zion Ministries
P.O.Box 34670 Kampala, Uganda
Email: return2zion@jesusanswers.com
Tel: +256 772 338 586

Scripture quotations taken from the HOLY BIBLE, NEW INTERNATIONAL VERSION (NIV) Copyright © 2011 by International Bible Society, used by permission; and AUTHORIZED KING JAMES VERSION (KJV) unless otherwise quoted.

This book has been published in print, e-format and sold on Amazon.com by:
KHAMEL Publishing
www.khamelpublishing.com

Publisher Contact:
P.O.Box 30532 Kampala
Email: melissakyeyune@gmail.com
Tel: +256 704 653 207

Acknowledgements

This book was conceived out of experience as God dealt with me, teaching me first to read His word, and then to apply it for victorious living. I have tried to best articulate all that I have learned over the years concerning the covenants of old and their application in a Christian's walk with God.

I wish to extend my sincere appreciation to Peter Ruhukya Asiimwe, whose support, input and testimonies have greatly enriched this work. Your friendship over the years has been invaluable. May God richly bless you.

I would like to appreciate Margaret Kisakye, my wife, for her support during the writing of this book. You have been a great companion through the years. May God continue to bind our hearts together.

I thank Elizabeth Asiimwe for her encouragement and patience during the writing of this book. Your support to Peter has been a great testimony to us.

Lastly, I extend my gratitude to my daughter, Monica Lakor, whom God used to make this project a reality. May God richly bless you for the touch you added to this book. I pray that through the content of this book, our lives will be changed, so that we enjoy a closer and more victorious walk with Jesus Christ!

Yours in Christ,
Nicholas Kisakye

Table of Contents

8

Introduction

This book is co-authored by Nicholas Kisakye and Peter Ruhukya Asiimwe. It includes personal testimonies of their walk with Christ and the lessons they have learned in living according to covenant promises.

Alvin Toffler, an American author of the last century said, "The illiterate of the 21st century will not be those who cannot read and write, but those who cannot learn, unlearn, and relearn."1 We therefore trust that as you read this book, you will continue learning, unlearning, and relearning new concepts as revealed by the Spirit of wisdom and revelation.

The purpose of this book is to demystify the covenants of God and how they can work in our lives on a daily basis.

Covenant Power Today:

The Divine Connection

NICHOLAS KISAKYE, PETER ASIIMWE

Chapter One

Lack of Knowledge Limits our Potential

For every first time, there is a 'not knowing'. Only by learning through experience or study does one gain understanding. Paul states that when he was a child, he thought like a child, but when he became a man, he thought like a man. The African belief is that age is a sign of wisdom. Peter's first flight experience may illustrate the perks of ignorance better.

Peter Asiimwe's first flight experience

It was a hot afternoon as Peter entered a plane for his first time ever. Peeping around to see how other passengers were fastening their belts he did the same. Soon the plane taxied out of Entebbe to Nairobi for the first leg to Harare. After a short while, he noticed air hostesses wheeling drinks through the aisles. Unfortunately, he did not have dollars and he knew that his Uganda shillings would not work on the plane. When the drinks reached him, despite the afternoon heat and the accompanying thirst, he sheepishly said "No, thank you". He arrived in Nairobi very thirsty indeed.

On the second leg to Harare, the following day a number of people he knew boarded Air Zimbabwe around 10:00 a.m. This time he felt more comfortable with the belts, and other security provisions as instructed by the air hostess. Around lunch time, smiling air hostesses wheeled lunch packages to different passengers. "Fish or chicken?", he could hear them asking passengers behind him. Feeling hungry and frustrated from having no money, but knowing that there were other passengers on the plane that knew him and could bail him out if he got into trouble, he resolved to eat the food no matter what! He had suffered enough on the first leg. He picked a plate of food, its sweet aroma filling his nostrils and ate it very quickly. On arrival in Harare, he disembarked with a sense of guilt, knowing that any time, someone would tap him for skipping the charge. To his surprise, no one seemed to notice his "offence". He later learnt that when one pays for a ticket, one is entitled to the food on the plane. Oh! How he regretted having missed his entitlements on the first leg. His thirst, and later his guilt, were due to his ignorance. He did not enjoy his benefits because of lack of knowledge. "My people perish for lack of knowledge." (Hosea 4:6)

Today, many people are living as spiritual paupers yet God has adequately provided for them everything they need for life and godliness through the knowledge of God and the covenant promises He has made (2Peter 1:3,4). Christians fail to live up to their expected potential due to ignorance. Paul speaking to Gentile Christians of Ephesus in Ephes. 2:11-13, said;

Therefore, remember that formerly you who are Gentiles by birth and called "uncircumcised" by those who call themselves "the circumcision" (that done in the body by the hands of men) -- [12] remember that at that time you were separate from Christ, excluded from citizenship in Israel and foreigners to the covenants of the promise, 9 without hope and without God in the world. [13] But now in Christ Jesus, you who once were far away have been brought near through the blood of Christ.

This passage surfaces three main problems of our past condition that deter many of us today from experiencing the full potential of what God has already provided for us.

No supply!

The first problem is that many are separated from Christ. They are disconnected from Christ the source of abundant life. The following example will help us understand the frustrations we often go through if we are separated or disconnected from the source of abundant life.

In August of 2011, Peter and I were invited to Hoima to speak at a mini-convention. We were accommodated in a guest house at the diocesan bishop's residence. Each one was given a room for the night. Peter woke up at about 5:00 a.m. but realised that we had no electricity. However, the guest house had an alternative source of power; solar panels connected to all rooms that were powered from, of all places, his room. He was surprised that even the solar power was not working in his room. In frustration, he made his way out of the room, only to find that all the other rooms had light. They were enjoying solar power, whose 'source' was in his room! At day break, he realised that the reason he had no power was due to a missing bulb. Though he had the source of power in his room, he was not connected to it. Many people live miserable lives because of being disconnected from Christ, the source of life.

Citizens-or not!

The second problem we see in Paul's message is that formerly, the Gentiles were excluded from the citizenship in Israel. They were aliens to the Commonwealth of Israel. The wealth of the Kingdom was not common or known to them.

Chapter Two

Laying the Foundation of Covenants in the Old Testament

Many times, God demonstrates a Kingdom principle in the Old Testament as a mirror image of a Kingdom principle for us to enjoy today. The Old Testament is often delineated from teachings today and rendered irrelevant by some theologians, and yet it is the foundation for the New Testament. For instance, the writer to the Hebrews said that the earthly sanctuary that was made in the Old Testament was only a copy or a type of the true one in heaven, and that that sanctuary was only an illustration for the present time (See Hebrews 9:9, 23,24).

Another is the Old Testament principle of having watchmen, gatekeepers, and gates (Isaiah 62:6,7), as a New Testament expectation for keeping watches as demonstrated by the Lord Himself (Matthew 14:25).

Another Old Testament example with spiritual significance for today was the Covenant box that God told Moses to construct as a symbol of God's presence in Israel's midst. Wherever the Covenant box would be, God's presence would be assured. Wherever the children of Israel went, God told them to keep it ahead of them as the assurance that God would be with them.

Whenever they went to war, the covenant box was with them. It enabled them to be guided in unknown paths. See this account of Israel as Joshua led the people to their divine destiny.

18

Joshua 3:1-4:
Early in the morning, Joshua and all the Israelites set out from Shittim and went to the Jordan, where they camped before crossing over. [2] After three days the officers went throughout the camp, [3] giving orders to the people: "When you see the ark of the covenant of the Lord your God, and the priests, who are Levites, carrying it, you are to move out from your positions and follow it. [4]Then you will know which way to go, since you have never been this way before. But keep a distance of about a thousand yards between you and the ark; do not go near it."

Whenever the Ark of the Covenant was ahead of them, a cloud would guide them by day and a pillar of fire by night. The cloud would protect them from the desert heat as they travelled, and the fire would light their path and warm them up in the night.

Numbers 10:33-34;
So they set out from the mountain of the Lord and travelled for three days. The ark of the covenant of the Lord went before them during those three days to find them a place to rest. [34] The cloud of the Lord was over them by day when they set out from the camp.

When they went to war, the Ark of the Covenant was ahead of them. The military strategy that God gave Joshua in taking Jericho had the Ark of the Covenant go before Israel to ensure victory.

Joshua 6:4-7:
Have seven priests carry trumpets of rams' horns in front of the ark. On the seventh day, march around the city seven times, with the priests blowing the trumpets. [5] When you hear them sound a long blast on the trumpets, have all the people give a loud shout; then the wall of the city will collapse and the people will go up, every man straight in." [6] So Joshua, son of Nun, called the priests and said to them, "Take up the ark of the covenant of the Lord and have seven priests carry trumpets in front of it." [7] And he ordered the people, "Advance! March around the city, with the armed guard going ahead of the ark of the Lord."

From these Old Testament examples, we can see God laying the foundation for kingdom-principle living today. We have seen that the Ark of the Covenant symbolised God's presence. It was instrumental in warfare. Above all, it helped guide Israel to possessing their inheritance in the Promised Land.

To understand the significance of the Ark of the Covenant further, let us now examine how it was constructed and glean lessons for today.

Chapter Three

The Elements of the Golden Covenant Box

When God wanted to teach a spiritual truth, He did things that the people could see and learn from. This way they saw His greatness, and learned His character. Having said this, we will now learn from the covenant box, its construction and contents. We will see what the Israelites needed to do before they could experience God's guidance, protection and provision. We will learn these things, so that we can have God's response reciprocated in our own lives today.

The Ark of the Covenant

The Ark of the Covenant was covered in gold. This signified the importance and worth of the elements that were kept inside the box. The principle of the less noble always protecting the more noble is at work here. The elements in the golden covenant box had more value than the gold which covered them. There were three main elements in the covenant box that have great significance even today. These included: the golden pot containing a piece of manna, the tablet stone of the Ten Commandments, and Aaron's almond rod.

As we shall soon see, we need to appreciate the fact that one who has, and depends on the Word of God for daily living, and is submissive to God's established leadership, has discovered more precious truths for living than one who has mere gold. He is richer than one who has large nuggets of gold. The one with gold might have discovered the art of making a living, whereas the one with the above precious truths has discovered the art of supernatural living. Let us now look at each element in the covenant box, and discuss its significance to enjoying covenant promises.

Manna in a golden pot

The manna was kept in a golden pot stressing further the importance and value of the manna. The Lord provided manna faithfully for the children of Israel on a daily basis as they went through the wilderness. These were the instructions given to Moses regarding the manna.

Exodus 16:16-22:
This is what the Lord has commanded: 'Each one is to gather as much as he needs. Take an omer for each person you have in your tent ..." [17] The Israelites did as they were told; some gathered much, some little. [18] And when they measured it by the omer, he who gathered much did not have too much, and he who gathered little did not have too little. Each one gathered as much as he needed. [19] Then Moses said to them, "No one is to keep any of it until morning." [20] However, some of them paid no attention to Moses; they kept part of it until morning, but it was full of maggots and began to smell. So Moses was angry with them. [21] Each morning everyone gathered as much as he needed, and when the sun grew hot, it melted away. [22] On the sixth day, they gathered twice as much - two omers for each person - and the leaders of the community came and reported this to Moses.

The Lord would provide manna daily for everyone. Israel was to depend on the Lord's promise to sustain them for each day. They were to learn that man does not live on bread alone but on every word that comes out of His mouth (Deut 8:3). If one took too much due to unbelief, it would rot.

The Lord told Moses to put a golden pot of manna in the Ark of the Covenant as a reminder and testimony of God's sovereignty (since the manna did not rot), and of His faithfulness in providing for His people.

God is faithful to do what He said he would do.

The manna proved God's faithfulness to His word. God would do as He said He would do. What would we pick from this as believers? That we need to take God's word and His promises to us in faith. Whenever He speaks, He does and whatever He promises, He fulfils!

Numbers 23:19 says this clearly:
God is not a man, that he should lie, nor a son of man, that he should change his mind. Does he speak and then not act? Does he promise and not fulfil?

Daily dependence on God and trust in His Word allows us to experience God's presence and guidance on a daily basis, even in the smallest things. We are victorious in all we do.

When we have learned, not just in our minds, but in our hearts, that God is faithful; He will do whatever He says He will do, we are said to have faith. A trust in His Word that is independent of everything else. A trust in His promises that is regardless of what we see in our present reality, regardless of what others say, even regardless of what makes logical sense, that is to say goes against the natural flow of things. This is faith. It is defined in Hebrews as the assurance of things hoped for.

Hebrews 11:1;
Now faith is being sure of what we hope for and certain of what we do not see.

It is a major theme in the word of God, and all God's people were shown to go through experiences that taught them and grew their faith. Sometimes these lessons were learned as a group of His people, other times it was individual. However, they all had opportunities to learn that God is faithful to those who put their trust in Him.

Isaiah 25:1;
O Lord, you are my God; I will exalt you and praise your name, for in

perfect faithfulness you have done marvellous things, things planned long ago.

Israel had their time of learning and experiencing God's faithfulness, and because of this, they made a decision to exalt and praise the Lord their God for the rest of their lives.

With today's global challenges of failing economies, inflation, natural disasters, poverty and other life issues that confront us, we need to learn that only by faith will the just live. (Habakkuk 2:4)

Ten Commandments in Stone

The stone tablet of God's Commandments was a symbol of the word of God or the Law. It was a reminder and representation of what God had taught the children of Israel; man does not live on bread alone, but on every word that comes out of His mouth (Deut 8:3). It is a sign of God's faithfulness to provide, to protect, heal and defend those who are obedient to His word and trust in every word that comes from His mouth. By His word, they would live.

When Moses was invited to lead Israel from Egypt, he realised that he could not do it. He saw the impossibility of leading close to a million people through a desert without water, food, clothes and so on. So he asked God how he could accomplish such a task. The Lord told him that He, the Lord, would be with Him. The most important resource that Moses would need to accomplish this task was God. It was not food, or water, or medicine, or even an army. It was God alone. God was sufficient. True to His Word, whenever there was a need, Moses turned to God who spoke to him in order to address the need. He became a way for them through the sea; food for them when they were hungry; water for them when they were thirsty; healer when they were bitten by serpents; pillar of fire to guide them by night and cloud to guide them by day. He even preserved their shoes and clothing, despite their 40 year journey. God was everything they needed. He became their all in all. They finally realised that whenever they had a need, God simply spoke. This showed that God was reigning through their lives and providing for their needs by His spoken word.

Even Jesus, the Word that became flesh, emphasised this through the living Word of God. He said, He is the Way, the Truth and Life. He is the Bread of life; the Living Water; He is our sufficiency.

Therefore, the commandments of God were a testimony of His dealing with His people. That through His word, He could reign in their lives and provide for every need they had.

The Mystery of the Almond!

Now, before discussing the significance of Aaron's rod in the Ark, we need to understand the symbolism of the almond tree. The word "almond" comes from the Hebrew word "shaqed" which means; wakefulness, alertness, sleeplessness, or hastening things.

The almond tree is the awake tree. It is the first to blossom in winter (February or even in late January) when all other plants or trees are still "asleep".The Lord used the symbolism of the almond tree to assure Jeremiah that He would fulfil His word and use Jeremiah to fulfil His purposes. Jeremiah had raised excuses on why he should not be called upon as a prophet.

He said, in *Jeremiah 1:6-12;*
"Ah, Sovereign Lord," I said, "I do not know how to speak; I am only a child." [7] But the Lord said to me, "Do not say, 'I am only a child.' You must go to everyone I send you to and say whatever I command you. [8] Do not be afraid of them, for I am with you and will rescue you," declares the Lord. [9] Then the Lord reached out his hand and touched my mouth and said to me, "Now, I have put my words in your mouth. [10] See, today I appoint you over nations and kingdoms to uproot and tear down, to destroy and overthrow, to build and to plant." [11] The word of the Lord came to me: "What do you see, Jeremiah?" "I see the branch of an almond tree," I replied. [12] The Lord said to me, "You have seen correctly, for I am

watching to see that my word is fulfilled."

The Lord put words in Jeremiah's mouth and with those words he appointed him to reign over nations, kingdoms, to uproot, tear down, destroy, and overthrow the kingdoms of darkness and all evil human endeavours. After that, Jeremiah was called to build and plant God's purposes and will on earth. He did this for his own life and for other people in the Kingdom of God.

God reigns through His Word, so He asked Jeremiah, "What do you see?" He said, "I have seen an almond tree" (an awake tree). To this, God responded saying that that he had seen correctly for He was awake and watching over His word to perform it. Just as the almond was awake, the LORD was awake to His Word and would ensure that it came to pass. In God's word, the almond tree is a symbol of watchfulness or alertness.

Another passage we can look at to understand the significance of the almond rod in the Ark of the Covenant is the prophetic action Jacob carried out to restore his fortunes from Laban. Jacob had been cheated and his wages changed ten times, but God was ready to restore his wealth in a supernatural way that spoke of God's sovereignty as the covenant keeping God. (Gen 31:6 -13) To restore his fortunes, Jacob used almond branches. Here is the account:

Gen 30: 37-43;
Jacob, however, took fresh-cut branches from poplar, almond and plane trees and made white stripes on them by peeling the bark and exposing the white inner wood of the branches. [38] Then he placed the peeled branches in all the watering troughs, so that they would be directly in front of the flocks when they came to drink. When the flocks were in heat and came to drink, [39] they mated in front of the branches. And they bore young that were streaked or speckled or spotted. [40] Jacob set apart the young of the flock by themselves, but made the rest face the streaked and dark-colored animals that belonged to Laban. Thus he made separate flocks for himself and did not put them with Laban's animals. [41] Whenever the stronger females were in heat, Jacob would place the branches in the troughs in

front of the animals so they would mate near the branches, [42] but if the animals were weak, he would not place them there. So the weak animals went to Laban and the strong ones to Jacob. [43] In this way, the man grew exceedingly prosperous and came to own large flocks, and maidservants and menservants, and camels and donkeys.

This is an illustration of the restoration of Jacob's fortune by God. We see the almond tree as a symbol of God's sovereignty and power in giving him increase. God chooses to do things the way He wants. We may, or may not understand it, but His way works. The natural way for plants is to bring leaves and then blossom. However, the almond tree is the only tree known to blossom before it brings out leaves. This also shows God's sovereignty. As we have already seen, while all other plants are asleep in winter, the almond is awake. It hastens to blossom first. Not only is the almond tree a symbol of God's sovereignty; it is also a symbol of God's watchfulness over His people (Ps 121). The almond illustrates God's sovereignty through His miracles and blessings. God moves and blesses His people and it usually gets spectators wondering 'How come?' In the incidences in which we see the almond evoke this kind of reaction, we like to refer to them as 'How come almond' blessings! How come, indeed!

We shall now look at another reason why the Aaron's almond rod was placed in the covenant box.

Numbers 16: 42- 17:13;
But when the assembly gathered in opposition to Moses and Aaron and turned toward the Tent of Meeting, suddenly the cloud covered it and the glory of the Lord appeared. [43] Then Moses and Aaron went to the front of the Tent of Meeting, [44] and the Lord said to Moses, [45] "Get away from this assembly so I can put an end to them at once." And they fell facedown. [46] Then Moses said to Aaron, "Take your censer and put incense in it, along with fire from the altar, and hurry to the assembly to make atonement for them. Wrath has come out from the Lord; the plague has started." [47] So Aaron did as Moses said, and ran into the midst of the assembly. The plague had already started among the people, but Aaron offered the incense and made atonement for them. [48] He stood between

the living and the dead, and the plague stopped. [49] But 14,700 people died from the plague, in addition to those who had died because of Korah. [50] Then Aaron returned to Moses at the entrance to the Tent of Meeting, for the plague had stopped. The Lord said to Moses, [2] "Speak to the Israelites and get twelve staffs from them, one from the leader of each of their ancestral tribes. Write the name of each man on his staff. [3] On the staff of Levi, write Aaron's name, for there must be one staff for the head of each ancestral tribe. [4] Place them in the Tent of Meeting in front of the Testimony, where I meet with you. [5] The staff belonging to the man I choose will sprout, and I will rid myself of this constant grumbling against you by the Israelites." [6] So Moses spoke to the Israelites, and their leaders gave him twelve staffs, one for the leader of each of their ancestral tribes, and Aaron's staff was among them. [7] Moses placed the staffs before the Lord in the Tent of the Testimony. [8] The next day, Moses entered the Tent of the Testimony and saw that Aaron's staff, which represented the house of Levi, had not only sprouted but had budded, blossomed and produced almonds. [9] Then Moses brought out all the staffs from the Lord's presence to all the Israelites. They looked at them, and each man took his own staff. [10] The Lord said to Moses, "Put back Aaron's staff in front of the Testimony, to be kept as a sign to the rebellious. This will put an end to their grumbling against me, so that they will not die." [11] Moses did just as the Lord commanded him. [12] The Israelites said to Moses, "We will die! We are lost, we are all lost! [13] Anyone who even comes near the tabernacle of the Lord will die. Are we all going to die?"

In this account, we see that Aaron's leadership was being disputed by Korah and his group of rebels. They wanted the priesthood (Numbers 16:1-14). After the destruction of Korah, God decided once for all to show Israel that the prevailing leadership had come from the Lord. As the passage shows, Aaron's almond staff budded and was kept as a continuous reminder to Israel that Aaron's leadership had its source from God. Any rebellion against established leadership draws God's disfavour and excludes us from enjoying covenant blessings.

In conclusion, we have seen that the almond tree is a symbol of God's sovereignty, and that He reigns in power and authority over His people.

He demonstrates His sovereignty in choosing to override the natural order of things as He gives us "How-come-almond-blessings". It is a symbol of God's alertness and watchfulness in fulfilling His Word. It is a symbol of protection since God always watches over His people. He neither slumbers, nor sleeps. It is a symbol of restoration of lost fortunes, and a symbol of God's choice of leaders, to whom we must submit, if we are to enjoy the promises of the covenant.

In Conclusion, we have seen that the three elements in the covenant box: the tablet of stone, the golden pot of manna and almond represent very important principles in the kingdom of God and they are more valuable than gold. That is why they were to be kept and preserved in a box made of pure gold.

We should live our lives according to the three principles represented by the elements in the covenant box:

• Trusting in the faithfulness of God towards His Word, especially in the area of provision – symbolised by the manna
• Knowing that man does not live on bread alone but on every word that comes out of the mouth of the Lord – symbolised by the stone tablet of the Ten Commandments.
• Appreciating God's sovereignty in restoring lost " fortunes" and in giving us "How-come-almond blessings",

His protection as He watches over His people and His Word, hastening its fulfilment; and realising that He and the leaders He chooses must be obeyed (except in the area of sin or rebellion against God) – symbolised by the Aaron's almond staff.

These three principles will guarantee God's presence and God's anointing on our lives. They will guarantee our protection and guidance, giving us hope and purpose as we dare to trust Him.

Chapter Four

The Power in the Covenants of God

In Genesis 17, when Abraham asked God how the promises would work for Him, God decided to make a covenant with him as an assurance that whatever God had said would be fulfilled for him. A covenant of God is made by God and is between Himself and man. Both parties have a part to play, and God's participation is conditional upon our fulfilment of our part. A covenant is stronger than a promise because where promises could be conditional in their fulfilment; covenants are enforced by an oath and carry undesirable consequences if not followed through. When God makes a covenant, He is bound by it and makes sure He fulfils what He has promised to do.

The writer to the Hebrews said in *Hebrews 6:13-18;*

When God made his promise to Abraham, since there was no one greater for Him to swear by, he swore by himself, [14] saying, "I will surely bless you and give you many descendants." [15] And so after waiting patiently, Abraham received what was promised. [16] Men swear by someone greater than themselves, and the oath confirms what is said and puts an end to all argument. [17]
Because God wanted to make the unchanging nature of his purpose very clear to the heirs of what was promised, he confirmed it with an oath. [18] God did this so that, by two unchangeable things in which it is impossible for God to lie, we who have fled to take hold of the hope offered to us may

be greatly encouraged.

The two unchangeable things in which it is impossible for God to tell a lie, are the oath, and the promise of His Word that is linked to His character.

Two Relevant Characteristics of God's Covenants

God remembers His covenants forever.

Psalm 111:5 ;
He provides food for those who fear him; he remembers his covenant forever.
From this scripture, we see the eternal nature of God's covenants.

God's provision for those who fear him is a covenant promise and the duration within which it is applicable is forever. We can trust this, because God's Word is binding. He is bound by it. That is why David said that he had never seen any servant of God or his children lacking what to eat. (Psalm 37:25)

As children of God, we should have no fear of lack according to this covenant promise.

This is a promise to sustain us with all we need. It is not about food alone, but about all that is needed to sustain us.

God's covenants are generational.

Our children benefit from their parents' blessings.

Psalm 112: 1-8;
Praise the Lord. Blessed is the man who fears the Lord, who finds great delight in his commands.[2] His children will be mighty in the land; the generation of the upright will be blessed. [3] Wealth and riches are in his house, and his righteousness endures forever. [4] Even in darkness light

dawns for the upright, for the gracious and compassionate and righteous man. [5] Good will come to him who is generous and lends freely, who conducts his affairs with justice. [6] Surely he will never be shaken; a righteous man will be remembered forever.[7] He will have no fear of bad news; his heart is steadfast, trusting in the Lord. [8] His heart is secure, he will have no fear; in the end he will look in triumph on his foes.

God Covenants are not only to bless an individual, but they are to bless his children, and their children, and not just them, but through the cross, even we can access them! God Remembers His Covenants Forever! Also Read 1Chronicles 16:15, 1Peter 1:23

Psalm 105:8-11:
He remembers his covenant forever, the word he commanded, for a thousand generations, [9] the covenant he made with Abraham, the oath he swore to Isaac. [10] He confirmed it to Jacob as a decree, to Israel as an everlasting covenant: [11] "To you I will give the land of Canaan as the portion you will inherit."

• God remembers His covenant forever and commands blessings for a thousand generations! (See Deuteronomy 7:9; 9:27).
• The covenant worked for Abraham who became a father of many nations.
• The covenant worked for Isaac who in time of hunger, planted seed and harvested a hundred fold because of the covenant (Genesis 26:12). He became exceedingly rich until even the king himself was scared of him.
• The covenant worked for Jacob whose fortunes were returned because of the covenant (Genesis 31:5-13). He had run away from his brother without anything and with no hope for the future. God gave him a vision in which he reminded him of the covenant he had made with his grandfather and assured him that it would work for him. Jacob himself believed in that covenant and made a vow that if God would protect, provide, and bless him, he would use the stone upon which he was lying as a foundation for the temple of God and he would pay a tithe of everything – out of gratitude (see Genesis 28).
• To Israel as an everlasting covenant. The covenant still works for

Israel as an everlasting covenant as it is today. Moses reminded Israel about God's purpose in their lives.

He said, *Deut. 8:6-18;*

Observe the commands of the Lord your God, walking in his ways and revering him. [7] For the Lord your God is bringing you into a good land - a land with streams and pools of water, with springs flowing in the valleys and hills; [8] a land with wheat and barley, vines and fig trees, pomegranates, olive oil and honey; [9] a land where bread will not be scarce and you will lack nothing; a land where the rocks are iron and you can dig copper out of the hills. [10] When you have eaten and are satisfied, praise the Lord your God for the good land he has given you. [11] Be careful that you do not forget the Lord your God, failing to observe his commands, his laws and his decrees that I am giving you this day. [12] Otherwise, when you eat and are satisfied, when you build fine houses and settle down, [13] and when your herds and flocks grow large and your silver and gold increase and all you have is multiplied, [14] then your heart will become proud and you will forget the Lord your God, who brought you out of Egypt, out of the land of slavery. [15] He led you through the vast and dreadful desert, that thirsty and waterless land, with its venomous snakes and scorpions. He brought you water out of hard rock. [16] He gave you manna to eat in the desert, something your fathers had never known, to humble and to test you so that in the end it might go well with you. [17] You may say to yourself, "My power and the strength of my hands have produced this wealth for me." [18] But remember the Lord your God, for it is he who gives you the ability to produce wealth, and so confirms his covenant, which he swore to your forefathers, as it is today.

In 2008, I (Peter) had the privilege of visiting Israel. True to God's Word, it is a blessed land! It is surrounded by strong enemies, but feared; with poor soils, yet exporting fruit worldwide including oranges, bananas etc. During our tour of Israel, one of our members asked the tour guide the secret of their good soils. The tour guide asked, "Which country are you from?" "Uganda." the inquirer responded. The tour guide said that they brought good top soil from Uganda as a result of excavations as they worked on the roads, airport, and buildings. They also imported banana stems from Uganda. They are now exporting agricultural produce. We, from Uganda were shocked by this. Israel took only a little soil and it is doing well in agriculture. We have the bulk of good soil and our people are dying of hunger. What a paradox. Could thriving on enduring covenant promises be the difference between Uganda's and Israel's fortunes?

God gives us assurance of His covenant promises;

Psalm 89:19-35;
Once you spoke in a vision, to your faithful people you said:"I have bestowed strength on a warrior; I have exalted a young man from among the people. [20] I have found David my servant; with my sacred oil I have anointed him. [21] My hand will sustain him; surely my arm will strengthen him. [22] No enemy will subject him to tribute; no wicked man will oppress him. [23] I will crush his foes before him and strike down his adversaries. [24] My faithful love will be with him, and through my name his horn will be exalted. [25] I will set his hand over the sea, his right hand over the rivers.[26] He will call out to me, 'You are my Father, my God, the Rock my Saviour.'
[27] I will also appoint him my firstborn, the most exalted of the kings of the earth.[28] I will maintain my love to him forever, and my covenant with him will never fail. [29] I will establish his line forever, his throne as long as the heavens endure. [30] "If his sons forsake my law and do not follow my statutes, [31] if they violate my decrees and fail to keep my commands, [32] I will punish their sin with the rod, their iniquity with flogging; [33] but I will not take my love from him, nor will I ever betray my faithfulness. [34] I will not violate my covenant or alter what my lips have uttered. [35] Once for all, I have sworn by my holiness - and I will not lie to David —

How can we know that God will do what He says He will do?

• We know that God can never violate His covenant. He is God.
• We know that He will never betray His faithfulness (see Numbers 23:19 and Heb 11:11)
• He swears by his holiness that he will not lie to David; Ps 89:35

To violate a covenant is to fail to adhere to what is expected from you or to fail to meet your end of the covenant. However, once God says something, it becomes law to him. He is bound by what He has spoken. He says, He will not violate His covenant or alter the word that goes forth from His mouth. That is why he has exalted His word and His Name above all things (Ps 138:2). He is always watching His Word to ensure it is fulfilled (Jeremiah 1:12) Many people though, think that this commitment was to David alone. This is not true! We can all dare to believe that what He says in this portion of scripture is for us!

Isaiah 34:16;
Look in the scroll of the Lord and read: None of these will be missing, not one will lack her mate. For it is his mouth that has given the order and his Spirit will gather them together.

Once he speaks, it is done!. It must come to pass.

Isaiah 55:1-4:
"Come, all you who are thirsty, come to the waters; and you who have no money, come, buy and eat! Come, buy wine and milk without money and without cost. [2] Why spend money on what is not bread, and your labor on what does not satisfy? Listen, listen to me, and eat what is good, and your soul will delight in the richest of fare. [3] Give ear and come to me; hear me, that your soul may live. I will make an everlasting covenant with you, my faithful love promised to David. [4] See, I have made him a witness to the peoples, a leader and commander of the peoples.

God is calling us to receive blessings from Him regardless of the weight of our wallets. If we listen to Him and depend on His word, we will eat what is good and our souls will delight in the richest of fare. He says that if we remain obedient to His word, He will make an everlasting covenant with us and His love, promised to David, will be ours. David is given as a witness to the peoples that we can depend on covenant promises. He who was faithful to David will be faithful to us.

Covenants and The Gentile

The covenants not only worked for Abraham, Isaac, Jacob and Israel; they also work for non Jews. The power in the covenants of God comes from the commitment that God has made and how he has bound himself to fulfil His covenants and the fact that when he makes a covenant, He remembers it forever. It will always work, and this is what gives it its eternal nature. The power is in the indestructible word.

Peter said, *1 Peter 1:23-25;*
For you have been born again, not of perishable seed, but of imperishable, through the living and enduring word of God. [24] For, "All men are like grass, and all their glory is like the flowers of the field; the grass withers and the flowers fall, [25] but the word of the Lord stands forever." And this is the word that was preached to you.

When we are born again through the Word of God, we are indestructible because we also receive the eternal nature of that word. Every word that God speaks is eternal and is loaded with power to work. It is like a guided torpedo. It has power for self-fulfilment. He is watching it to fulfil it. The nature of the word of God gives us an imperishable nature.

As we read it and obey and put our trust in it, it empowers us with God's anointing and constantly transforms our nature so that devils are put under our feet.

As we have already seen, these covenants also work for Gentiles. They will therefore work for whoever believes in them. We read in *Ephesians 2: 13-14* that we are no longer excluded from the citizenship of Israel.

We have been brought in, to be members of God's family. In Christ Jesus we can freely and boldly access what God has covenanted to do for his children. We are no longer excluded from the covenants He made to Israel.

Paul speaking to the Galatians (non Jewish believers) said in *Galatians 3:15-16;*

Brothers, let me take an example from everyday life. Just as no one can set aside or add to a human covenant that has been duly established, so it is in this case. [16] The promises were spoken to Abraham and to his seed. The Scripture does not say "and to seeds," meaning many people, but "and to your seed," meaning one person, who is Christ.

Paul continues to assure the Galatians, Jews, and non Jews that through Christ, they have a share in the blessings of God through the covenants. It is through the "seed" that we too share in the covenant promises.

Galatians 3:26-29;
You are all sons of God through faith in Christ Jesus, [27] for all of you who were baptized into Christ have clothed yourselves with Christ. [28] There is neither Jew nor Greek, slave nor free, male nor female, for you are all one in Christ Jesus. [29] If you belong to Christ, then you are Abraham's seed, and heirs according to the promise.

This simply means that if you belong to Christ, then you are Abraham's seed and should enjoy the promises.

Chapter Five

The Relationship Between the Covenants, the Law, and the Grace through the Cross

We need to understand the chronological order of events in God's plan. He begins with the covenants to Abraham, then the Law and then He reveals Grace. Why does the Law come in between the covenants of God and grace?

Paul speaking to the Galatians said, Galatians 3:17-25;
What I mean is this: The law, introduced 430 years later, does not set aside the covenant previously established by God and thus do away with the promise. [18] For if the inheritance depends on the law, then it no longer depends on a promise; but God in his grace gave it to Abraham through a promise. [19] What, then, was the purpose of the law? It was added because of transgressions until the Seed to whom the promise referred had come. The law was put into effect through angels by a mediator. [20] A mediator, however, does not represent just one party; but God is one. [21] Is the law, therefore, opposed to the promises of God? Absolutely not! For if a law had been given that could impart life, then righteousness would certainly have come by the law. [22] But the Scripture declares that the whole world is a prisoner of sin, so that what was promised, being given through faith in Jesus Christ, might be given to those who believe. [23] Before this faith came, we were held prisoners by the law, locked up until faith should be revealed. [24] So the law was put in charge to lead us to Christ that we might be justified by faith. [25] Now that faith has come, we are no longer under the supervision of the law.

The first thing we see in this passage is that the Law has an important role to play in the life of a believer. It reveals our sinfulness. It is like a mirror in which we look and are able to see our sin. It also judges us and condemns us so that we are able to see our helplessness and hopelessness without God.

The second thing we see from this passage is that the whole world is first held as a prisoner to sin, so that what was promised being given through faith in Jesus Christ might be given to those who believe. Paul continues with this same argument in *Romans 3:20-23* when he says that through the Law we become conscious of sin and that all have sinned and fallen short of the glory of God. The law points us to the need for a new righteousness apart from the law: a righteousness that comes by grace through faith. It points and leads us to the cross of Christ.

Without feeling guilty and condemned by the law you cannot understand and find true grace. God's grace is found at the Cross. The Cross is a point of weakness. But it is also at the Cross that we find God's grace - the divine connection to God's unlimited power. When we come to the end of our resources, we come to the beginning of God's resources.

The Cross is God's gift to the Church but rarely do Christians appreciate its significance. Many appreciate the role of the blood of Jesus for the washing away of sin but very rarely do they appreciate the Cross. Yet, in Col 2:15, Paul tells us that it is at the cross that Jesus disarmed the powers of darkness and accessed the power that raised him from the grave. Without appreciating what Jesus did for us on the Cross and believing in it, we can never find the power to defeat the devil.

In the Old Testament, The Lord said to Moses,

Numbers 21:8-9;
"Make a snake and put it up on a pole; anyone who is bitten can look at it and live." [9] So Moses made a bronze snake and put it up on a pole. Then when anyone was bitten by a snake and looked at the bronze snake, he lived.

That serpent is a symbol of Jesus Christ on the Cross. When we look at Him and meditate on what he obtained for us on the Cross, we are able to access the power that defeats the powers of darkness and heals us from the effects of sin. The Cross is not for the strong but for the weak. It is where the defeated go to find God's power.

When we realise what Christ has achieved for us through the Cross, we draw grace which empowers the covenants in the Old Testament that were made to the "seed".

Every covenant, is connected to a relevant promise that God gave us when Jesus died on Cross. Because God is just, His Kingdom principles operate on a legal framework. He neither violates His covenant nor alters the word that comes out of his mouth. Therefore, we need to stand on the legal ground of Calvary (where justice, grace and love meet) to access the covenants in the Old Testament.

At the Cross, we accessed a divine exchange. Because of the Cross:

• Jesus died, that we may live.
• He was punished, that we may be forgiven.
• He was wounded, that we may be healed.
• He was rejected, that we may be accepted.
• He became a curse (Galatians 3:11-13) that we may be blessed along with Abraham who was blessed in all things. (Genesis 24:1)
• He became sin, that we may be clothed with His righteousness.
• He became poor (in thirst, and nakedness), that we may be made rich.
• He was broken, that we may be made whole.
• He took our shame that we may share in His glory.
• He became a prisoner, that we may be free.
• He went to hell that we may go to heaven.

All the blessings of this divine exchange are provided for in the covenant promises God made to Abraham that through him, all the nations of the world would be blessed. Through the seed (Jesus), we share in the covenant blessings.

In summary, the law was given to make us aware of sin and to point us to the cross. This is because justification by observance of the law was impossible. On the cross, we connect with the covenants made to Abraham and his seed. We are no longer strangers to those covenants for there is neither free nor slave, female or male, Jew or Gentile in Christ.

Some covenant promises that can work for us today.

Deut. 7:12-15
If you pay attention to these laws and are careful to follow them, then the Lord your God will keep his covenant of love with you, as he swore to your forefathers. [13] He will love you and bless you and increase your numbers. He will bless the fruit of your womb, the crops of your land - your grain, new wine and oil - the calves of your herds and the lambs of your flocks in the land that he swore to your forefathers to give you. [14] You will be blessed more than any other people; none of your men or women will be childless, nor any of your livestock without young. [15] The Lord will keep you free from every disease. He will not inflict on you the horrible diseases you knew in Egypt, but he will inflict them on all who hate you.

From this scripture, we see the following covenant promises that we could enjoy:
• If we are obedient to His laws, then He will keep his covenant of love with us. He will never break it.
• He will bless us and increase our numbers
• He will bless the fruit of our womb. Now, to many, this means our children only. But if one has no children, it can also mean that God will bless our reproductive systems to enable us get children. That is why He says in verse 14 that none of your men or women would be childless. Not even our livestock will be without the young. This covenant promise will break the curse of barrenness even as far as our livestock is concerned.
• He will bless the crops of our land, our grain and oil. In other words, He will bless our agricultural potential even dealing with the devourers of our crops.

He will keep us free from every disease. Every disease means every disease. No disease is left out. This is in line with Ps 103:2 where He says that He forgives us all our sins and heals all our diseases. He will not inflict on us horrible diseases of Egypt, but He will instead inflict them on our enemies who are warned not to touch the Lord's anointed.

Psalm 112: 1-8;
Praise the Lord. Blessed is the man who fears the Lord, who finds great delight in his commands.[2] His children will be mighty in the land; the generation of the upright will be blessed. [3] Wealth and riches are in his house, and his righteousness endures forever. [4] Even in darkness light dawns for the upright, for the gracious and compassionate and righteous man. [5] Good will come to him who is generous and lends freely, who conducts his affairs with justice. [6] Surely he will never be shaken; a righteous man will be remembered forever.[7] He will have no fear of bad news; his heart is steadfast, trusting in the Lord. [8] His heart is secure, he will have no fear; in the end he will look in triumph on his foes.

Look at all the promises that we can benefit from.

• The children of a man who fears the Lord are destined to be mighty in the land. The word "mighty" comes from a Hebrew word "gibbowr", which means powerful champions, valiant warriors, strong leaders with a spirit of excellence upon them. We can position our children for success by tapping into these generational covenant blessings.
• The assurance of rich provision in one's house
• Many other promises that we can glean from these verses and can energize our prayer.

Leviticus 26:1-13
"Do not make idols or set up an image or a sacred stone for yourselves, and do not place a carved stone in your land to bow down before it. I am the Lord your God. [2] " 'Observe my Sabbaths and have reverence for my sanctuary. I am the Lord. [3] "'If you follow my decrees and are careful to obey my commands, [4] I will send you rain in its season, and the ground

will yield its crops and the trees of the field their fruit. [5] Your threshing will continue until grape harvest and the grape harvest will continue until planting, and you will eat all the food you want and live in safety in your land. [6] "'I will grant peace in the land, and you will lie down and no one will make you afraid. I will remove savage beasts from the land, and the sword will not pass through your country. [7] You will pursue your enemies, and they will fall by the sword before you. [8] Five of you will chase a hundred, and a hundred of you will chase ten thousand, and your enemies will fall by the sword before you. [9] " 'I will look on you with favour and make you fruitful and increase your numbers, and I will keep my covenant with you. [10] You will still be eating last year's harvest when you will have to move it out to make room for the new. [11] I will put my dwelling place among you, and I will not abhor you. [12] I will walk among you and be your God, and you will be my people. [13] I am the Lord your God, who brought you out of Egypt so that you would no longer be slaves to the Egyptians; I broke the bars of your yoke and enabled you to walk with heads held high.

See this covenant promises to claim:

• He will send us rain and the ground will yield its crops.
• He will give us an abundant harvest.
• He will give us peace and we will lie down and have nothing to fear. This is a promise against fear, doubt, and discouragement.
• He will remove savage beasts from the land – this includes demons that molest us.
• He assures us of victory against our enemies.
• He will grant favour upon our lives.
• We will still be eating last year's harvest when we will have to move it out to make room for the new. These are promises of abundant blessings and no lack at all.
• He will put His dwelling presence among us. This is an assurance of God's constant presence wherever we are.
• We will not be enslaved again. This is a promise of redemption from Satanic enslavement and deliverance from every yoke of the enemy. This speaks about all enemies including political, spiritual, social, economic

and all other enemies.

Isaiah 34:16; 17
Look in the scroll of the Lord and read: None of these will be missing, not one will lack her mate. For it is his mouth that has given the order, and his Spirit will gather them together. He allots their portions; his hand distributes them by measure. They will possess it forever and dwell there from generation to generation.

• We have a promise from God to give us mates for marriage. This is an order from the mouth of God and because it is so, God's Spirit will make sure that he will bring them together.

• He has also given the promise to give us our inheritance in marriage and to possess it from generation to generation. This is a promise of continuity and passing on an inheritance for our children.

Isaiah 49:24-25
Can plunder be taken from warriors, or captives rescued from the fierce? 25] But this is what the Lord says: "Yes, captives will be taken from warriors, and plunder retrieved from the fierce; I will contend with those who contend with you, and your children I will save.

This covenant promise is ours to claim.

• When our children are taken as captives, they can be delivered from drugs, immorality, rebellion, and other forms of bondage.

• We can stand on the finished work of Christ to legally restore what the locusts have eaten. We can reverse the course of events as Jacob did through the almond prophetic action. The covenant will lead us to our inheritance.

Testimonies from Today Attesting To God's Divine Power in us

Nicholas Kisakye's testimony

By 1991, my business, which had previously been very successful, had been completely destroyed and I was serving as a volunteer in the Province of the Church of Uganda in the mission department. Because of the increasing financial demands on my family, I decided to pull out of the mission work to either look for a job or to go back into business. It was because of this decision that I realised I had lost the joy of salvation and it seemed like I was carrying a big burden on my shoulders. This was a sign that I had made a wrong decision. I then declared a dry fast for three days in order to find out what God's will was.

After the fast, God gave me a dream, which I could not interpret. I prayed and asked Him to speak more clearly to me. In the morning, when I had gone to pick my children from school, I heard a clear voice telling me to read *Isaiah 58 verse 11*.

"The Lord will guide you always; he will satisfy your needs in a sun-scorched land and will strengthen your frame. You will be like a well-watered garden, like a spring whose waters never fail".

From this scripture, I realised that God had assured me of provision even if I was in a desert. He would strengthen and heal me and I would not only be constantly blessed but I would be anointed to continue being a blessing to the Church without running dry. I was overwhelmed and excited because I knew God had answered me. I believed this promise and started praying it into our lives every morning. And God opened doors of divine provision.

Since then, I have established a faith ministry (Return to Zion Ministries) and God has faithfully provided for us as a family and for the ministry. God has healed us from sicknesses including healing me from mental sickness that I suffered from for seven years.

When I saw the promise in *James 1:5-6*

"If any of you lacks wisdom, he should ask God, who gives generously to all without finding fault, and it will be given to him. [6] But when he asks, he must believe and not doubt, because he who doubts is like a wave of the sea, blown and tossed by the wind." ,

My wife and I started to pray for our children, asking God for this kind of wisdom to excel academically and for wisdom to make good decisions in life. God helped our children to excel. In fact, one of our children was the best in her Primary Leaving Examinations in Uganda. She was also among the very best in Ordinary Level (High School) exams in the country. Because of her outstanding performance, she got a scholarship and to do an International Bachelorette Diploma abroad. As I write (September 2011), she is attending at one of the best universities in the world abroad on yet another scholarship. It has been a successful walk of faith, not only for her education, but for every one of our children's. The Lord has kept His Word to us, over and over again!

God has done many other miracles to prove His faithfulness and I have also seen many people healed and delivered during ministry as these principles have been taught.

When I learned these truths, I started teaching other believers the use of the promises of God in the areas of provision, protection and healing. One day, as I was preaching to a brother in the Lord, he felt convicted to become born again. (He will be referred to as Sam to protect his privacy) However, he had a problem. He had run away from a war zone and his salary was too small to support his family of 13 people. Because of this, his wife took to brewing local beer and working in a local bar to supplement their income. He wondered how he would sustain the family if he became born again. It would require him to stop his wife from doing what she did for work.

Immediately, the Lord gave me a scripture from *John 15:7,*

"If you remain in me and my words remain in you, ask whatever you wish, and it will be given you."

Sam realised that this was said by Jesus Himself and that it was possible for Christ to do that for him. He therefore asked Christ to come into his life and save him. Then he went and asked his wife to stop doing whatever she was involved in. His wife thought he was crazy and assured him that there was no way he would look after the family with his little salary, if she stopped brewing alcohol. But she stopped.

After a few days the food reserves in his house were done and his wife brought him the bad news. "This is our last meal," she said. Sam prayed, reminding God of the promise He had made to Him and then went to attend the fellowship meeting in Church, believing God for a miracle.

During the meeting, nothing eventful happened. However, as he came out of the Church, an elderly woman talked to him and said that from the moment she had seen him, she had felt it on her heart to bless him with 400 Uganda shillings (about 1/7 of a US dollar then). When Sam saw the money, his hopes were further dashed because that money could only buy half a kilogram of maize flour at that time. He decided to take the money to his wife so that she would buy some porridge for dinner. As he was returning to his work place, he found soldiers sharing maize flour, so he decided to give that little money to them in exchange for some maize flour. It was at this time that the supervisor of the soldiers saw him talking to them and became concerned as to why this civilian was talking to his soldiers. In fear, Sam explained his predicament to their boss who empathised with him, instructing the soldiers to give him 100 kilograms of maize flour and 60 kilograms of beans. He told the men to carry it to his home. When his wife saw him coming with men carrying food ahead of him, she too believed God and asked Christ to save her.

From that day, Sam claimed that scripture, John 15:7, and every time he did, he received miracles. Today all his children are graduates, some with Masters Degrees; he has a beautiful house and is now a manager for one of the radio stations in the country. His salary has been multiplied over many times.

These testimonies and many others put us on the path of realising that God is faithful to do whatever He has promised to do for us in His word. The word of God has taken on different meanings in our lives. We are living by the Word from His mouth.

Peter Ruhukya Asimwe's Testimony

One evening of April 1985, while in Nairobi, Kenya attending the Campus Crusade new staff training with Life Ministry, I was burdened and began to weep because of the condition of the Church back home in Uganda. We were not taking God by His Word. There was a lot of unbelief. I pleaded with God to use me to the maximum to help accelerate the Great Commission (Matthew 28:18-20). While still weeping, I went to bed and God spoke to me through a very clear dream. Through the various scenes of the dream, He made these clear;

• I was not to be afraid of death from the increased dangers of working in the city. He had the enemy (the queen of death) under control.
• He would supply everything I needed in order to serve Him.
• He said audibly that, "Be strong and of good courage, for you shall cause many people to inherit the Promised Land". He further said, "Go and read *Joshua 1:3*"

I woke up from the dream and read the book of Joshua beginning with *Joshua 1:3*

"Every place the soul of your foot will tread upon, I have given it to you".

I read further through verse 6

Be strong and of good courage, for you shall cause many people to inherit the Promised Land.

I was very thrilled to learn that what I had heard audibly was the Word of God.

I asked the LORD what He meant by "causing many people to possess the Promised Land". I discovered that in helping to accelerate the Great Commission, I would help many individuals, families, communities and nations realise their divine destinies in God.

Later, in 1986, I started reading the book of Exodus and Numbers and realised that the same God who took Israel through the great and terrible wilderness, providing and protecting them, was the same God that I had. If He could dress, feed, guide, and protect Israel in a desert, then He could do the same for me in Uganda. Having learnt that to join Life Ministry Uganda, one lives by faith trusting God for daily needs, I and my wife took the opportunity to let God demonstrate His faithfulness in providing, protecting, and guiding us.

Prior to joining this ministry, I had worked as an Industrial Chemist, and as a secondary school teacher. I left all this to serve God, who said He would protect me and provide for all our needs.

The LORD has given us both biological and non biological children, none of whom has ever reported late to school or university for lack of fees. Since we started serving Him twenty years ago, the Lord has faithfully met each of our needs! We have experienced miraculous provision.

One evening, a man we thought was a thief brought us several bunches of bananas. We had prayed to God, asking Him to give us our daily needs. We have received miraculous healing. One time as we were praying, the Lord removed a bad heart from my wife and gave her a new one with new blood vessels. That was the end of Pectoris Angina, a condition that doctors had diagnosed condemning her to life-long expensive medication. I too received a new heart through miraculous intervention.

At one time in the city, someone took my briefcase. It had very valuable things including my office keys. I remember that when we reached home, we stood at our family altar and prayed that we would recover our brief case. The following day, we got it intact. When I lost my mobile phone, again we prayed at the family altar reminding God of how He had intervened in the briefcase saga. The following day, I asked my wife to go and report the case to our local council chairman. He laughed at her wondering why she had bothered to do so. On her way from his home, the chairman called her back. Someone had just dropped the phone off at his home.

I have had opportunities to travel to several countries in Africa, in Europe, in the Far East, to Russia, and to the USA, sharing the gospel.

Our God never changes. He is the same yesterday, today and forever. He is the God of the covenant. Whatever He says He will do, He does.

Chapter Six

Dealing with Old Satanic Covenants in Order to Benefit from God's Covenants

To help us understand how we can benefit from God's covenants, we shall look at the way God established his covenant with Abraham. We shall also see how Gideon dealt with his father's wrong satanic foundations in order to benefit from God's calling on his life. First, a look at Abram's calling while he lived in Haran.

Gen 12:1-3;
The Lord had said to Abram, "Leave your country, your people and your father's household and go to the land I will show you. [2] "I will make you into a great nation and I will bless you; I will make your name great, and you will be a blessing. [3] I will bless those who bless you, and whoever curses you I will curse; and all peoples on earth will be blessed through you."

Why does God tell Abram to make such a costly sacrifice of leaving his people and his country? What was the issue? To understand this, let us examine the background to this passage by looking at the account of Terah, the father of Abram.

Genesis 11:27-32;54
This is the account of Terah. Terah became the father of Abram, Nahor and Haran. And Haran became the father of Lot. [28] While his father Terah was still alive, Haran died in Ur of the Chaldeans, in the land of his

birth. [29] Abram and Nahor both married. The name of Abram's wife was Sarai, and the name of Nahor's wife was Milcah; she was the daughter of Haran, the father of both Milcah and Iscah. [30] Now Sarai was barren; she had no children. [31] Terah took his son Abram, his grandson, Lot son of Haran, and his daughter-in-law, Sarai, the wife of his son Abram, and together they set out from Ur of the Chaldeans to go to Canaan. But when they came to Haran, they settled there. [32] Terah lived 205 years, and he died in Haran.

From this account we can make the following observations:

1. Abram's family was knitted together. They moved together. His father Terah had other sons, Nahor and Haran, the father of Lot.

2. When Haran died, Abram took care of Lot, his brother's son. This was a caring family.

3. Terah takes his son Abram, his grandson Lot, and his daughter-in-law, Sarai, to go from Ur of the Chaldeans to Canaan. Is this a coincidence that Terah was being called to go to Canaan where Abraham was also called to go? It looks like the calling of God was first on Terah, Abraham's father, but when he reached Haran, he did not continue to Canaan. He settled there and died there!

Why did Terah settle in Haran? Many people get callings from God but settle down before their callings are realised. In order to understand this challenge, let us look at what Joshua said, *Joshua 24:1-3*;

Then Joshua assembled all the tribes of Israel at Shechem. He summoned the elders, leaders, judges and officials of Israel, and they presented themselves before God. [2] Joshua said to all the people, "This is what the Lord, the God of Israel, says: 'Long ago, your forefathers, including Terah the father of Abraham and Nahor, lived beyond the River and worshiped other gods. [3] But I took your father Abraham from the land beyond the River and led him throughout Canaan and gave him many descendants.

The context of this passage is at a point when the children of Israel have crossed over into the Promised Land and Joshua is urging them to renew their covenant with God if they are going to be blessed in the land of promise. However, before they make the new covenant, Joshua is reminding them of wrong foundations which had been laid in the past.

He tells them that long ago, their forefathers, including Terah, the father of Abram, lived beyond the River and worshipped other gods. Here we see that Terah did not continue in God's calling but settled in Haran and died there because of idolatry.

No one can fulfil his or her destiny in God unless he or she first disconnects himself or herself from idolatry, renouncing it, and establishing a new covenant with God.

An idol is anything that is exalted or exalts itself above God. This could be in one's thoughts or actions, or in how much time and attention it takes from one. It is anything that an individual believes in and puts one's trust in, fully depending on it. One may consciously pray to it, or sub consciously rely on it, more than they do God. In the end, it comes between them and God. They cannot fully depend on God because their trust lies elsewhere.

God takes idolatry very seriously. He hates it in whatever form it manifests itself. That is why God required Abram to disconnect himself from his father's idolatry, from his country, from his family, and from his people that he dearly loved. It was not an easy thing for Abram to do; that is why he wandered about with Lot, but God could not bless him until he had eventually separated himself from Lot. (see Gen 13)

Many people limit idolatry to outright satanic worship or witchcraft, but the broader understanding of idolatry includes everything that takes first place before God. This could include our spouses, children, jobs, money, pleasure, and the like.

Here, we see Joshua reminding Israel of their past, a past that was built on wrong foundations. He tells them of how God had been faithful to bless them, but takes them to task to make a choice to serve the Lord only.

He said, *Joshua 24:14-15;*
"Now fear the Lord and serve him with all faithfulness. Throw away the gods your forefathers worshiped beyond the River and in Egypt, and serve the Lord. [15] But if serving the Lord seems undesirable to you, then choose for yourselves this day whom you will serve, whether the gods your forefathers served beyond the River, or the gods of the Amorites, in whose land you are living. But as for me and my household, we will serve the Lord."

Joshua challenges the people to make a personal choice and commitment to do away with idolatry in order to serve the Lord. He is not challenging others only; he too makes the same commitment with his family. The scripture shows that the people responded hastily without thinking deeply about the implications of their choice.

Joshua 24:16-18;
Then the people answered, "Far be it from us to forsake the Lord to serve other gods! [17] It was the Lord our God himself who brought us and our fathers up out of Egypt, from that land of slavery, and performed those great signs before our eyes. He protected us on our entire journey and among all the nations through which we travelled. [18] And the Lord drove out before us all the nations, including the Amorites, who lived in the land. We too will serve the Lord, because he is our God."

Then Joshua said to the people, *Joshua 24:19-20;*
"You are not able to serve the Lord. He is a holy God; he is a jealous God. He will not forgive your rebellion and your sins. [20] If you forsake the Lord and serve foreign gods, he will turn and bring disaster on you and make an end of you, after he has been good to you."

Joshua made the people realise that it is not easy to serve the Lord because of two main reasons:

He is a holy God.

He is a jealous God.

We too need to be reminded that to serve the Lord and to enjoy His covenant blessings, we need to deal with idolatry and serve the Lord only. Gideon's example as one who had to deal with wrong foundations in order to enjoy God's blessings for himself and the whole nation will help us underscore this.

Judges 6:1-28;

Again the Israelites did evil in the eyes of the Lord, and for seven years he gave them into the hands of the Midianites. [2] Because the power of Midian was so oppressive, the Israelites prepared shelters for themselves in mountain clefts, caves and strongholds. [3] Whenever the Israelites planted their crops, the Midianites, Amalekites and other eastern peoples invaded the country. [4] They camped on the land and ruined the crops all the way to Gaza and did not spare a living thing for Israel, neither sheep nor cattle nor donkeys. [5] They came up with their livestock and their tents like swarms of locusts. It was impossible to count the men and their camels; they invaded the land to ravage it. [6] Midian so impoverished the Israelites that they cried out to the Lord for help. [7] When the Israelites cried to the Lord because of Midian, [8] he sent them a prophet, who said, "This is what the Lord, the God of Israel, says: I brought you up out of Egypt, out of the land of slavery. [9] I snatched you from the power of Egypt and from the hand of all your oppressors. I drove them from before you and gave you their land. [10] I said to you, 'I am the Lord your God; do not worship the gods of the Amorites, in whose land you live.' But you have not listened to me." [11] The angel of the Lord came and sat down under the oak in Ophrah that belonged to Joash the Abiezrite, where his son Gideon was threshing wheat in a winepress to keep it from the Midianites. [12] When the angel of the Lord appeared to Gideon, he said, "The Lord is with you, mighty warrior." [13] "But sir," Gideon replied, "if the Lord is with us, why has all this happened to us? Where are all his wonders that our fathers told us about when they said, 'Did not the Lord bring us up out of Egypt?' But now the Lord has abandoned us and put us into the hand of Midian." [14] The Lord turned to him and said, "Go in the strength you have and save Israel out of Midian's hand. Am I not sending

you?"[15] "But Lord," Gideon asked, "how can I save Israel? My clan is the weakest in Manasseh, and I am the least in my family."
[16] The Lord answered, "I will be with you, and you will strike down all the Midianites together." [17] Gideon replied, "If now I have found favor in your eyes, give me a sign that it is really you talking to me. [18] Please do not go away until I come back and bring my offering and set it before you."And the Lord said, "I will wait until you return." [19] Gideon went in, prepared a young goat, and from an ephah of flour he made bread without yeast. Putting the meat in a basket and its broth in a pot, he brought them out and offered them to him under the oak.
[20] The angel of God said to him, "Take the meat and the unleavened bread, place them on this rock, and pour out the broth." And Gideon did so. [21] With the tip of the staff that was in his hand, the angel of the Lord touched the meat and the unleavened bread. Fire flared from the rock, consuming the meat and the bread. And the angel of the Lord disappeared. [22] When Gideon realized that it was the angel of the Lord, he exclaimed, "Ah, Sovereign Lord! I have seen the angel of the Lord face to face!" [23] But the Lord said to him, "Peace! Do not be afraid. You are not going to die." [24] So Gideon built an altar to the Lord there and called it The Lord is Peace. To this day it stands in Ophrah of the Abiezrites. [25] That same night the Lord said to him, "Take the second bull from your father's herd, the one seven years old. Tear down your father's altar to Baal and cut down the Asherah pole beside it. [26] Then build a proper kind of altar to the Lord your God on the top of this height. Using the wood of the Asherah pole that you cut down, offer the second bull as a burnt offering." [27] So Gideon took ten of his servants and did as the Lord told him. But because he was afraid of his family and the men of the town, he did it at night rather than in the daytime. [28] In the morning when the men of the town got up, there was Baal's altar, demolished, with the Asherah pole beside it cut down and the second bull sacrificed on the newly built altar!

Gideon comes on stage when the nation of Israel is in slavery because of their sin. They cried to God who calls Gideon to deliver them. Let us see what we learn from this passage.

1. The angel tells Gideon that the Lord is with him as a mighty warrior.

This suggests that he was in the right standing with God and that he was mightly anointed to serve God. He tells him to go in the strength of God's might to set Israel free from slavery. (see Judges 6:13,14)

2. Gideon raises an altar to the Lord in order to worship God and to receive peace from Him for Israel (Judges 6:24). Here we need to realise that Gideon was accepted before God like any born again believer today would be accepted.

3. However, God did not accept the altar that Gideon built. Why?

• Gideon had behind him a satanic altar erected by his father, which altar was still speaking in his life. This is in line with the teaching in Exodus 20:1-6 where God commands Israel not to set up any idol. God warned that He would visit in judgement whoever engages in idolatry even to the third and fourth generation of their children. Accordingly, Gideon was reserved for judgment and there was no way he could draw from God's blessings unless he first dealt with and repented of the sin of his father. That is why God told him to destroy his father's altar first, then and only then would he be in position to build a proper altar for God.

• Moreover, for every physical or spiritual marriage, there are records or certificates that are written. For example, in Psalms 106:28, Israel yoked itself spiritually with the Baal of Peor and ate sacrifices offered to lifeless god's hence provoking God to anger. Records of this spiritual prostitution speak in our lives. They need to be renounced and dealt with. (Colossians 2:14)

What God asked Gideon to do was a serious matter and it scared him. But he knew that to walk in the blessings of God, he had to do it. He got ten friends that would be likened to intercessory partners in today's language, to help him destroy the altar.

From the moment Gideon destroyed his father's altar and erected a proper one for God, we see God's favour on him. He had victory upon victory in every war he fought until the whole nation of Israel was delivered from slavery.

Conclusion

We have seen that many Christians live without hope because of their lack of knowledge regarding the covenant promises that God made to Abraham and his seed. We have shown the connection between those Covenants, the Law, and the Cross. We have argued that the law is good because it makes us aware of our own helplessness. It points us to the Cross where we are given our freedom, and entitlement to the covenants and the promises for God's people in the Word.

The Word of God is not just a story book, but is the best thing that God has given humanity. When we realise all that God has availed for us within His written Word, and realise that we can stand on it to receive all that we need for life and godliness, we are ushered into God's will for victorious living. God will not lie. His word is eternal, and will not return to Him Void. It must do that which He sent it forth to do, even today! It was not just for the Israelites, or for the priests and preachers, not even for the scholars and philosophers of old alone! Its power is available to all of us today! We can begin to live victoriously today! This is not to say it is a tool for manipulation of God or a 'to do' list for Him. If we can determine to read it with the realisation of its power constantly on our minds, we can keep our end of the bargain, as we prayerfully and in humility ask God for and remind Him of His.

Deuteronomy 32: 45-47;
When Moses finished reciting these words to all Israel, He said to them,
" Take to heart all the words I have solemnly declared to you this day, so
that you may command your children to obey carefully all the words of
this law. They are not just idle words for you, they are your life. By them
you will live long in the land you are crossing the Jordan to possess."

May God open our eyes to the magnitude of power in His word, and to the reality of its being as effective and available to us today, so that its truth may be to our faith what yeast is to bread! Closed books never open the mind. Read! Believe! Conquer! Today!